SIENCE FI

ANCIENT
ALIENS

DID HISTORIC CONTACT HAPPEN?

RACHAEL L. THOMAS

**Checkerboard
Library**

An Imprint of Abdo Publishing
abdopublishing.com

ABDOPUBLISHING.COM

Published by Abdo Publishing, a division of ABDO, PO Box 398166, Minneapolis, Minnesota 55439.
Copyright © 2019 by Abdo Consulting Group, Inc. International copyrights reserved in all countries.
No part of this book may be reproduced in any form without written permission from the publisher.
Checkerboard Library™ is a trademark and logo of Abdo Publishing.

Printed in the United States of America, North Mankato, Minnesota
052018
092018

THIS BOOK CONTAINS
RECYCLED MATERIALS

Design: Emily O'Malley, Mighty Media, Inc.
Production: Mighty Media, Inc.
Editor: Jessie Alkire
Cover Photographs: Shutterstock
Interior Photographs: Alamy, pp. 9, 24; iStockphoto, pp. 5, 7, 19, 21, 28 (bottom right), 29; NASA, p. 27; Shutterstock, pp. 13, 15, 16, 23, 28 (left), 28 (top right); Wikimedia Commons, p. 11

Library of Congress Control Number: 2017961621

Publisher's Cataloging-in-Publication Data
Names: Thomas, Rachael L., author.
Title: Ancient aliens: Did historic contact happen? / by Rachael L. Thomas.
Other titles: Did historic contact happen?
Description: Minneapolis, Minnesota : Abdo Publishing, 2019. | Series: Science fact or
    science fiction? | Includes online resources and index.
Identifiers: ISBN 9781532115370 (lib.bdg.) | ISBN 9781532156090 (ebook)
Subjects: LCSH: Extraterrestrial beings--Juvenile literature. | Human-alien encounters--
    Juvenile literature. | Answers to questions--Juvenile literature. | Science fiction in
    science education--Juvenile literature.
Classification: DDC 001.942--dc23

CONTENTS

On June 22, 1941, American professor Paul Kosok went on a research trip in the desert region of southern Peru. He was hoping to better understand the region's natural water systems. Along the way, Kosok investigated mysterious lines in the sand.

Kosok likely heard about these lines from airplane pilots. Kosok wondered if the lines could have been used for ancient **irrigation** or as a calendar. Kosok and German archaeologist Maria Reiche studied the lines for many years. Many other archaeologists soon followed.

These researchers hoped to map the lines. The only way to do so was to view the lines from above. From high in the sky in an airplane, the lines could be seen more clearly. The lines stretched across the desert for hundreds of miles. Some of the lines were perfectly straight across hills and rocky ground. As researchers mapped the lines, they realized the lines formed **geometric** patterns and

There is now an observation deck near the Nazca Lines so people can climb up and see the lines from above.

These lines were the Nazca Lines. They were created almost 2,000 years ago. The Nazca Lines could only be truly appreciated from the sky. But air travel was not possible in ancient times. So, who could the Nazca Lines have been drawn for? Could the lines have been used to communicate with alien spacecraft?

WHAT ARE ANCIENT ALIENS?

Today, many people believe that life exists beyond Earth. Some scientists are even trying to locate other life forms across the universe. But ancient alien theorists believe contact with aliens first occurred long ago.

Ancient alien theorists think aliens arrived on Earth thousands of years ago. This alien contact with humans shaped modern life. Theorists say there is evidence of alien contact in ancient writing and **architecture**.

There is a growing interest in ancient aliens among the public. But ancient aliens remain a **controversial** topic. Archaeologists and other experts believe ancient alien theorists misrepresent science and history.

Scientists have been researching human history for many centuries. But no one can be sure how civilizations arose, thrived, or failed. Ancient aliens are a way to potentially solve these mysteries. Believers ask that people stay open-minded and ask questions. Are ancient aliens real? Did historic contact happen?

Ancient alien theorists look for evidence of alien contact in art and even in carvings on buildings.

Ancient alien theory has become popular in recent years. But the possibility of an ancient alien visit was first proposed almost a hundred years ago. Between 1928 and 1932, Russian scientist Nicholas Rynin wrote the book *Interplanetary Contacts.* In it, he explored the role of aircraft in ancient legends. These legends included Ancient Greek myths and Hindu stories. Rynin proposed that the origins of such stories may be more fact than myth.

In 1968, Swiss author Erich von Däniken published a book called *Chariots of the Gods.* The book discussed ancient aliens. It was a breakthrough publication for the theory. The book sold millions of copies worldwide. Since then, von Däniken has become a well-known expert in ancient alien theory. He has traveled around the world to talk about his beliefs.

Scientists today are rallying to **debunk** the ancient alien theory. Still, the theory's popularity is growing.

The History Channel **debuted** a TV series, *Ancient Aliens*, in March 2009. The series explores ancient alien theory. It was intended to be a two-hour special. But it became so popular among viewers that the show was extended for many seasons!

Erich von Däniken's books have sold more than 60 million copies worldwide!

ANCIENT STORIES

People have studied ancient myths and legends for centuries. Many experts believe that learning about past fictional writing is vital. It helps both historians and ancient alien theorists learn about ancient societies.

Ancient alien theorists believe these stories could be fact rather than fiction. Ancient texts often speak of visits from gods or other supernatural beings. Theorists suggest that certain texts are records of alien visits!

One example is Greek myths. The earliest Greek myths were recorded around 800 to 700 BCE. Greek myths discuss ancient gods. The gods are often described riding chariots. Theorists believe these gods were actually **extraterrestrials**. And their chariots were UFOs!

Ancient alien theorists also think mythical beasts could have extraterrestrial explanations. Many of these beasts have body parts from multiple animal species. One example is the Minotaur. This was a legendary creature with the head of a bull and the body

Greek mythology discusses a monster called Medusa. She looked like a normal woman but had snakes for hair!

of a man. Ancient alien theorists believe the Minotaur and other beasts were real creatures. Theorists think **extraterrestrials** created these monsters by combining animal species with genetic engineering or other **technologies**.

Other ancient texts have been used to support the ancient alien theory. Some of the most famous are the Sumerian epics. These are long poems written by people from Sumer.

The region of Sumer was in what is now southern Iraq. Sumer was first settled between 4500 and 4000 BCE. It is the earliest known civilization in ancient history. Ancient texts discuss Sumerian mythology.

Sumerian myths describe a group before humans called the Anunnaki. The Anunnaki were a race of gods that worked as laborers on Earth. They were controlled by more powerful gods. One day, the Anunnaki grew tired of the hard work they were performing, so they **rebelled**. They fought against the gods with fire and an "evil wind." Then the Anunnaki created a new race to continue their hard labor. This new race was humankind.

In 1976, American author Zecharia Sitchin published a book on ancient aliens called *The 12th Planet.* In it, he proposes that parts of Sumerian myths refer to **extraterrestrials**. He references the myth of the Anunnaki.

Sumerian myths were often carved into clay or stone slabs. Sumerians used a system of writing called cuneiform, in which words were represented by drawings or symbols.

Sitchin's book claims that the Anunnaki myth is based in fact. Sitchin argues that the Anunnaki were **extraterrestrials**. They genetically engineered humans to do their work. Sitchin also says the fire and wind of the Anunnaki's **rebellion** resembled nuclear warfare. This is used as evidence of advanced extraterrestrial **technology**.

Ancient alien theory doesn't end with ancient stories. It also includes ancient art and **architecture**. All over the world, archaeologists have discovered ancient monuments, statues, and buildings. These discoveries often show a high level of skill and artistry. But ancient alien theorists question how ancient civilizations created these structures.

Many ancient structures are made from huge pieces of rock. These pieces are called megaliths. Today, engineers use advanced **technologies** to remove and transport heavy rock. But ancient structures were built before these technologies were invented.

An example of an ancient structure is the Great Pyramid of Giza in Egypt. The Great Pyramid

FOR REAL?

Humans could recreate the Great Pyramid today using construction **vehicles**, cranes, and helicopters. Experts think it would take five years to build. And it would cost $5 billion!

was built around 2560 BCE. It is made of 2.3 million stone blocks. The average weight of each stone block is between 2 and 15 tons (1.8 and 13.6 t)!

Ancient alien theorists question how these heavy blocks were removed, formed, and transported. Theorists think alien visitors taught or lent **technologies** to the ancient Egyptians. Then the Egyptians used the technologies to build the Great Pyramid.

The Great Pyramid was used as a tomb for a powerful Egyptian king, Khufu.

The explanation for the Great Pyramid can be extended to other structures too. Puma Punku is an ancient ruin. It is near Lake Titicaca in western Bolivia. The site is about 1,500 years old.

Some of the stone blocks at Puma Punku form the letter *H*. The stones interlock so perfectly that a needle cannot be inserted between them!

Puma Punku is an incredible example of ancient engineering. The largest stone block at the site weighs 144 tons (131 t)! The stone blocks are cut into **geometric** shapes that perfectly interlock. And the surfaces of some stones are so smooth that they feel like glass.

Giorgio A. Tsoukalos is a well-known ancient alien theorist. He has studied Puma Punku. When Puma Punku was built, tools were simple. Tsoukalos doesn't think these tools could have been used to build Puma Punku. Instead, Tsoukalos believes that Puma Punku was built using alien **technology**.

Tsoukalos also says a local legend proves his ancient alien theory. According to Tsoukalos, Spanish colonizers asked local people how Puma Punku was built. The locals told the Spaniards of a legend. The legend said that Puma Punku was built in one night by the gods.

Tsoukalos believes this legend is rooted in fact. He thinks that the gods mentioned in the legend were alien visitors. These **extraterrestrials** built Puma Punku, not people or gods.

While many ancient alien theories are based on elaborate structures, some also reference simpler physical evidence. One example is the Nazca Lines. They are located about 200 miles (322 km) south of Lima, Peru.

The Nazca Lines are **geoglyphs**. They were **etched** into the desert earth between 1,500 and 2,000 years ago. Local tribes removed the dark upper layer of rock from the ground. This exposed the paler sand underneath. The local people drew hundreds of lines. In total, the lines cover 310 square miles (803 sq km).

The Nazca Lines were discovered by Peruvian archaeologist Toribio Mejia Xesspe in 1926. He saw the Nazca Lines while walking. Soon after, travel by airplane became more common.

FOR REAL?

One Nazca geoglyph forms the shape of a pelican. It is the length of three football fields!

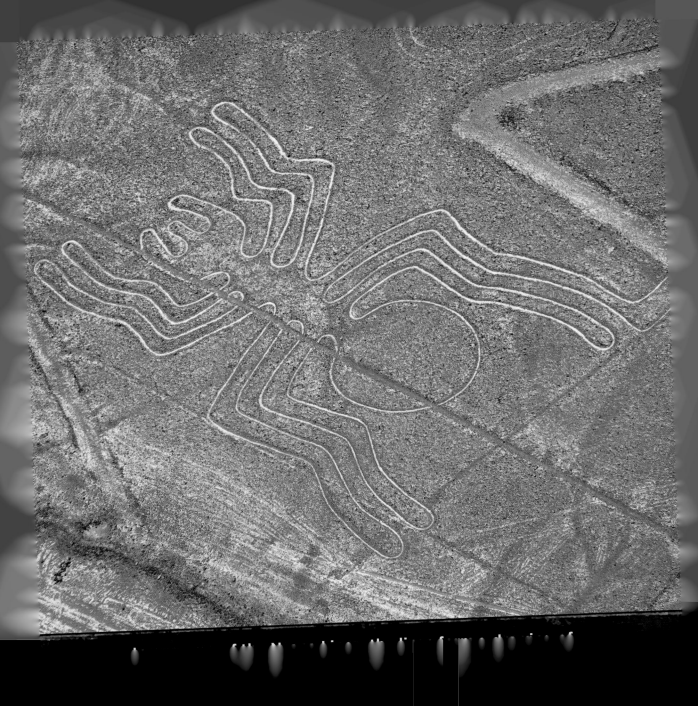

From the air, the Nazca Lines looked completely different. People in airplanes could see the lines formed patterns and drawings. Some of the drawings were of animals, such as hummingbirds and monkeys.

Unlike many ancient structures, the Nazca Lines would not have been difficult to create. The ancient tribes of Peru could have easily made the lines with basic tools. But scientists are uncertain of the origin and purpose of the Nazca Lines.

Ancient alien theorists believe the Nazca Lines were created to be seen from the air. But air travel was not possible when the Nazca Lines were made. So, theorists have suggested that Peruvian tribes used the lines to signal alien spacecraft. Others believe the lines are a map or landing field for **extraterrestrial** visitors.

David Childress is an ancient alien theorist. He calls attention to a Nazca drawing referred to as "The Spaceman." This drawing is a human-like figure. Childress says The Spaceman appears to be wearing a space helmet. He believes that the drawing was created in the likeness of past alien visitors!

Name:
- The Nazca Lines, "The Spaceman"

Location:
- The desert of South Peru, near the village of Nazca

Claims:
- Message left for **extraterrestrials**
- Resemblance to alien life-form

Evidence:
- Human-like shape
- Appears to be wearing a space helmet
- One arm up as though waving
- Viewed clearly only by aircraft

Status:
UNSOLVED

Ancient alien theories offer explanations for mysteries that scientists can't explain. But ancient aliens are just one possible solution. Scientists develop other theories based on scientific and historic knowledge.

Researchers have offered alternative explanations for the Nazca Lines. They believe the lines were likely created for religious **rituals**. The desert landscape of southern Peru is very dry. So, local tribes could have held rituals to pray to the gods for rain. This would explain why the lines are best viewed from the heavens.

Scientists also refute Sitchin's **analysis** of Sumerian myths. Sitchin compares the "evil wind" described in the ancient text to a nuclear blast. He uses this as evidence of alien **technology**. But scientists claim that the myth could refer to a sandstorm or wildfires.

Researchers also believe ancient alien theory underestimates ancient people's abilities. Alien theorists argue that if a task is difficult today, it would have been

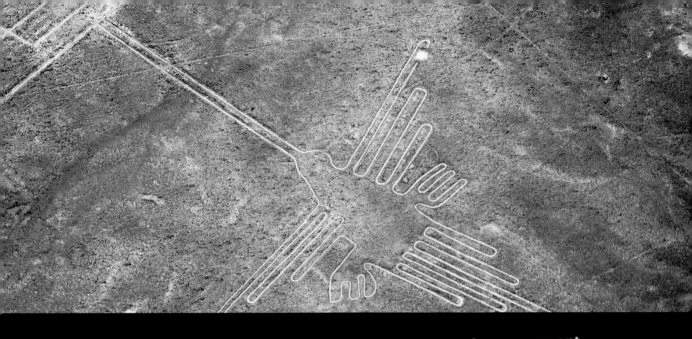

Researchers believe some of the Nazca Line drawings represent symbols. For example, hummingbirds are a sign of fertility.

impossible in the past. But researchers believe people in ancient times were as intelligent as people today.

For example, ancient Egyptians developed building skills and tools over hundreds of years. They made **sledges** to transport stone from nearby **quarries**. Thousands of workers helped build the Great Pyramid. Researchers think these factors are much more likely than **extraterrestrial** help.

Erich von Däniken (*left*) and Giorgio A. Tsoukalos (*right*) have been featured on the *Ancient Aliens* TV series.

Almost all qualified scientists reject the idea of ancient aliens. It is an area of study that is often considered **pseudoscience**. So, alien theorists receive very little support from the scientific community.

This is partly because even the best-known alien theorists are not scientists. Von Däniken is the leading figure in ancient alien theory. But he isn't a scientist. For many years before publishing *Chariots of the Gods*, he ran a hotel in Switzerland.

Von Däniken, Sitchin, and other theorists are accused of cherry-picking. This means that they use information that supports their theories and ignore information that doesn't. Scientists think ancient alien theorists cherry-pick images from art and ignore cultural **context**. For example, many theorists believe a carving in a Mayan tomb shows an alien in a spacecraft. But experts in Mayan religious symbols say the drawing represents a deceased Mayan king moving into the underworld.

However, ancient alien theorists accuse scientists of cherry-picking too. They think scientists only believe in explanations that fit with modern science. It is unlikely that scientists and ancient alien theorists will agree on explanations for certain **phenomena**. But both groups continue to form theories to explain the world's many mysteries.

Ancient alien theory has not been proven. But there are still questions about human history that scientists have yet to answer. Ancient aliens are becoming a popular way to address these mysteries. A survey conducted by Chapman University in California found that 35 percent of Americans believe that aliens visited Earth in the distant past.

Most scientists are quick to dismiss ancient alien theory. However, many respected scientists believe in some form of alien life beyond Earth. Scientists don't know where aliens might be or what they could be like. But new **technologies** might help scientists find out!

High-powered telescopes now allow researchers to see

FOR REAL?

Scientists planned the launch of the James Webb **infrared** space telescope in 2018. They hope its cameras will be able to detect light from stars and galaxies while they are forming.

many millions of miles into space. Using these telescopes, scientists have discovered distant galaxies, stars, and planets. According to **NASA**, between 10 and 20 percent of stars have Earth-sized planets orbiting them. These planets might support alien life. If alien life is possible today, then could ancient aliens have existed too?

In 2017, NASA announced that its Kepler Space Telescope discovered an eighth planet orbiting Kepler-90. Kepler-90 is a star 2,545 light-years from Earth.

4500–4000 BCE
The region of Sumer is settled by the first known human civilization.

2560 BCE
The Great Pyramid is built in ancient Egypt.

800s–700s BCE
The earliest Greek myths are written.

1926
The Nazca Lines are discovered by Peruvian archaeologist Toribio Mejia Xesspe.

1928–1932
Russian scientist Nicholas Rynin writes *Interplanetary Contacts*. In it, he analyzes aircraft in Greek mythology.

1968
Swiss author Erich von Däniken publishes a book about ancient aliens, *Chariots of the Gods*.

1976
American author Zecharia Sitchin publishes *The 12th Planet*. It discusses the relationship between ancient aliens and Sumerian myths.

2009
The *Ancient Aliens* TV series premieres on the History Channel.

2018
The James Webb space telescope launch is planned.

YOU DECIDE!

Did ancient alien contact happen? You decide!

- Read books and articles about ancient alien theories.
- Watch the TV series *Ancient Aliens* on the History Channel.
- Study planets, galaxies, and other space topics.
- Explore archaeology and history topics to find out about ancient cultures and architecture.

GLOSSARY

analysis—the identification or study of the parts of a whole.

architecture—the art of planning and designing buildings.

context—the circumstances that form the setting or understanding for an event or idea.

controversial—of or relating to a discussion marked by strongly different views.

debunk—to prove wrong or false.

debut—to make a first appearance.

etch—to make a pattern or design on a hard surface.

extraterrestrial—coming from beyond Earth. Someone or something from beyond Earth is called an extraterrestrial.

geoglyph—a large image or design created on the surface of the earth.

geometric—made up of straight lines, circles, and other simple shapes.

infrared—related to a type of light that people can't see.

irrigation—the watering of plants or crops, usually by channels or artificial means.

NASA—National Aeronautics and Space Administration. NASA is a US government agency that manages the nation's space program and conducts flight research.

phenomena—facts or events that are rare or extraordinary.

pseudoscience—theories that are not based in science.

quarry—a place where stone is cut or blasted out for use in building.

rebel—to resist or disobey authority. The act of resisting or disobeying is a rebellion.

ritual—a ceremony or form of worship that follows a specific procedure or order.

sledge—a sled or other vehicle that is pulled to transport a load.

technology—scientific tools or methods for doing tasks or solving problems.

vehicle—something used to carry or transport. Cars, trucks, airplanes, and boats are vehicles.

ONLINE RESOURCES

Booklinks
NONFICTION NETWORK
FREE! ONLINE NONFICTION RESOURCES

To learn more about ancient aliens, visit **abdobooklinks.com**. These links are routinely monitored and updated to provide the most current information available.